J
520
SI

Sipiera, Paul P.

I can be an
astronomer

$12.60

DATE		
JY 22 '91	DE 3 '92	MAY 30 '96 · JE 05 '06
AG 12 '91	AP 23 '93	JL 1 '96 · AG 11 '08
FE 12 '92	APR 7 '94	JUN 30 '97 · NV 11 '12
MR 13 '92	JUL 22 '94	AG 25 '97 · JY 26 '18
AP 1 '92	DEC 01 '94	SEP 24 '98 · OC 04 '18
AP 20 '92	DEC 20 '94	NOV 06 · AP 17 '18
MY 11 '92	MAR 29 '95	DEC 18 '98 · JE 24 '19
JY 28 '92	JL 11 '95	JY 03 00
AG 13 '92	SEP 01 '95	
OC 29 '92	FEB 29 '96	MY 04 01
NO 10 '92	APR 25 '98	JY 09 01

I CAN BE AN
ASTRONOMER

By Paul P. Sipiera

Prepared under the direction of Robert Hillerich, Ph.D.

 CHILDRENS PRESS ®

CHICAGO

Library of Congress Cataloging-in-Publication Data
Sipiera, Paul P.
  I can be an astronomer
  (I can be)
  Summary: Discusses the work that astronomers do as
they study the stars to learn more about the universe.
  1. Astronomy—Vocational guidance—Juvenile
literature. 2. Astronomy—Juvenile literature.
[1. Astronomy—Vocational guidance. 2. Vocational
guidance. 3. Occupations] I. Title. II. Series.
QB51.5.S57   1986   520'.23   86-9629
ISBN 0-516-01883-3

3 4 5 6 7 8 9 10 11 R 95 94 93 92 91 90 89 88 87

PICTURE DICTIONARY

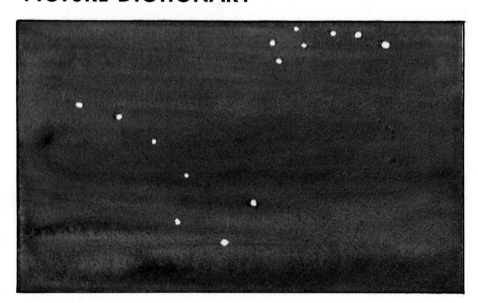

constellation

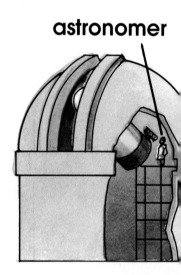

observatory

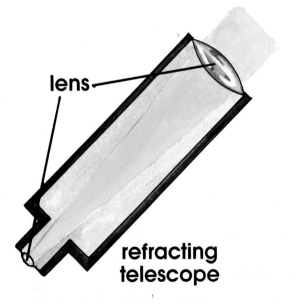

refracting telescope

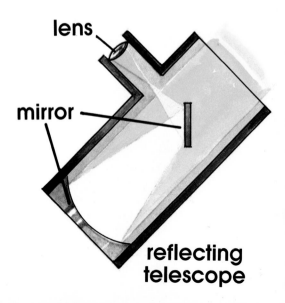

reflecting telescope

planetarium

comet

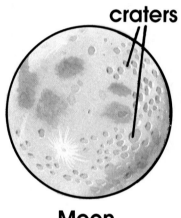

craters

Moon

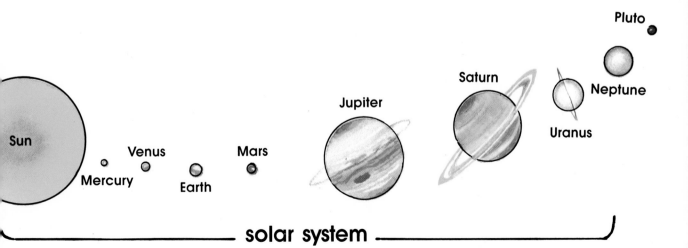

Sun

Mercury

Venus

Earth

Mars

Jupiter

Saturn

Uranus

Neptune

Pluto

solar system

Astronomers explore the mysteries of the night sky.

Have you ever seen the stars at night? Did you wonder what they are? People who study the stars are called astronomers.

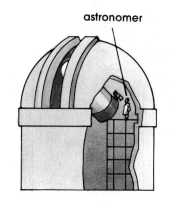

astronomer

Long ago astronomers learned to use the heavens to calculate

Above: At Stonehenge in England, ancient people built these monuments as a gigantic calendar. By viewing heavenly bodies through openings in the stones, they could measure periods of time. Below: This observatory, built in India in 1726, was used to observe the skies and to tell time.

time. They made calendars to help farmers grow their crops. They measured the day, the month, and the year by observing the sky.

constellation

The sun is used to measure a day. The moon's cycle of changes gives us the month. Patterns of stars called constellations are used to measure a year.

Moon

The ancient Maya people of Mexico built this observatory at Chichen Itza.

Knowledge of the heavens is very important. Early sailors learned to navigate by using the constellations. These bright stars were the basis of many stories and legends. Some of

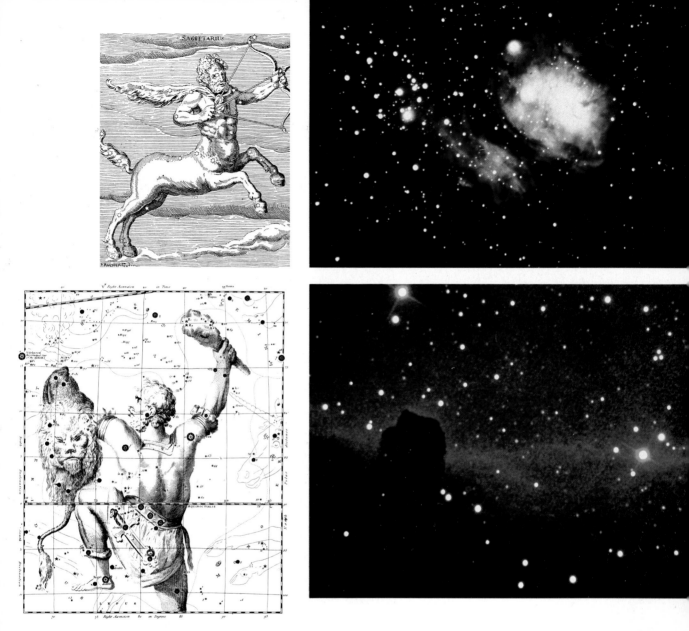

The constellations Sagittarius (top left and right) and
Orion (bottom left and right), in legend and in reality

them were given the
names of ancient gods
and heroes.

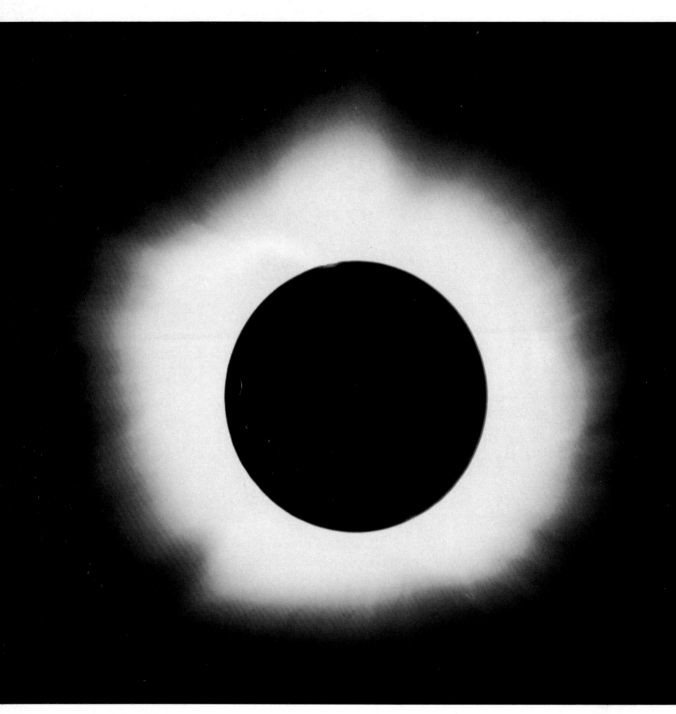

In this solar eclipse of March 7, 1970, the moon totally blocked out the
sun for three and a half minutes. In a solar eclipse, the moon comes between
the Earth and the sun.

One job for the astronomer is to predict eclipses. During a solar eclipse the sun turns dark. When the bright full moon turns dark, we have a lunar eclipse. Eclipses once caused great fear. But ancient astronomers learned how to predict eclipses. Then people no longer had to fear them.

Today astronomers study the stars to learn more about the universe. They use powerful telescopes to see far out into space. A telescope makes objects look bigger and brighter.

There are many different kinds of telescopes. A refracting telescope uses a lens to gather in light. A reflecting telescope uses

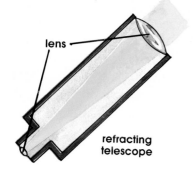

lens

refracting telescope

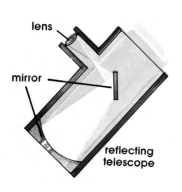

lens

mirror

reflecting telescope

Above: The Naval Observatory in Washington, D.C.
Left: A refracting telescope with a 26-inch diameter
Below: Viewing the sky from an observatory

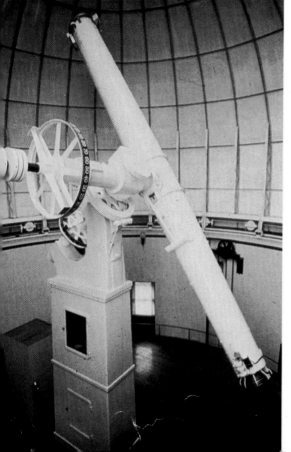

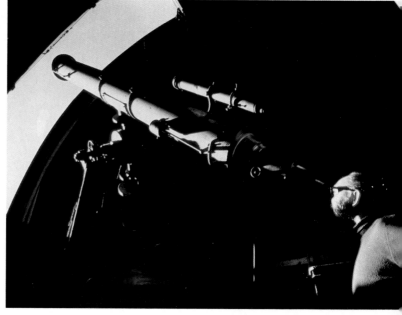

a mirror. Both collect
light from the stars and
planets.

Stars, such as our own
sun, send out light.
Planets reflect sunlight
just like the moon does.

A radio telescope
does not use visible light.
It collects invisible forms
of energy. The
temperature of space
can be taken with a
radio telescope. It can
be used day or night.

The radio telescope at Parkes Observatory in Australia, 210 feet (64 meters) in diameter

Other astronomers use
a spectroscope to study
the stars. This instrument
can tell how old a star is.
It can also measure how
far away from us it is. It
can tell what the star is
made of.

Most astronomers do not look through a telescope. They use a camera to photograph the stars. The camera collects more light than the human eye. Astronomers now make most of their discoveries by examining photographs. This is how the planet Pluto was discovered.

This early camera (left) used sunlight to enlarge and print pictures. The telescope at McDonald Observatory at Ft. Davis, Texas (right) is 108 inches in diameter.

Astronomers who use telescopes work in observatories. These buildings are placed high atop mountains, where the air is clear

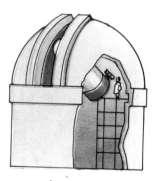

observatory

Kitt Peak National Observatory in Arizona

and the sky is dark.
Astronomers work in
observatories from sunset
to sunrise on cloudless
nights.

Not all astronomers
work at observatories.

An astronomer teaching children about the stars at a planetarium

Some work at planetariums. Others teach at universities. A few astronomers even go into space aboard the space shuttle. One day

planetarium

Saturn's rings are made of particles of matter that circle it.

an astronomer will work
on the moon. Some astronomers
study the planets. They

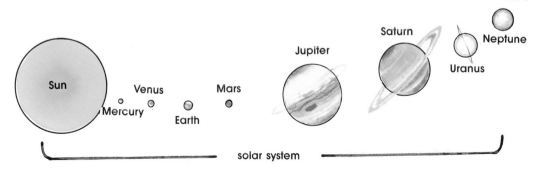

 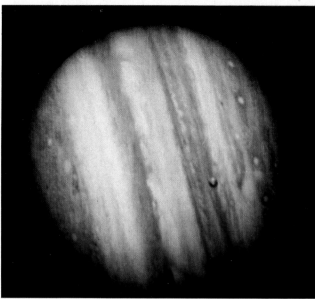

Mars (left) is similar to Earth in many ways. Jupiter (right) has sixteen satellites, or moons.

study the rings of Saturn and the moons of Jupiter. Mars has always been an interesting planet. It has polar ice caps and river channels like Earth has. Perhaps a form of life may exist there.

This moon rock, nicknamed "Big Bertha," was brought back to Earth by *Apollo 14*.

Others who study the planets look at weather patterns on Venus and Jupiter. Or they search for volcanoes on Mars. Some study moon rocks and meteorites.

A meteorite found near Odessa, Texas

Meteorites are pieces
of iron and rock that fall
from space. Most come
from an area between
Mars and Jupiter called
the asteroid belt. They
provide clues to the
origin of our solar system.

Moon rocks were carried back to Earth by the astronauts. They are older than any Earth rock. Someday scientists will once again explore the moon. Many of the other planets will be explored too. Perhaps you may be one of these scientists.

Astronomers also search the sky for comets. Comets are

comet

Comet Ikeya-Seki

often called "dirty
snowballs." They are
made of ice and dust. A
comet is named after
the person who
discovers it. The most
famous comet is named

This 1910 photograph of Halley's comet was reconstructed by computer to show different levels of brightness with colors.

after Edmond Halley. This comet visits the Earth about every seventy-five years.

How can you become an astronomer? It takes many years of study.

McDonald
Observatory's
82-inch-diameter
telescope

Mathematics and
physics are important
subjects to learn.

There are many good
books to help you learn
about the stars. A trip to
a planetarium will show

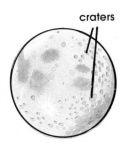
craters

you all the nighttime
stars. A small telescope
will show you craters on
the moon and the
moons of Jupiter.

A career in astronomy
can be exciting. Perhaps
someday you may go to
Mars and look back at
the Earth. The future
belongs to you!

WORDS YOU SHOULD KNOW

asteroid belt (AST • er • oyd BELT)—an area between Mars and Jupiter where thousands of small planets are in orbit

calculate (KAL • kyoo • late)—to figure out by measuring or using mathematics

comet (KAH • mitt)—a heavenly body composed of ice and dust that shows a long, glowing tail when near the sun

constellation (kahn • stell • AY • shun)—a grouping of stars that appears to form a familiar pattern in the sky

crater (KRAY • tur)—a large, bowl-shaped hole made by a falling meteor

eclipse (ee • KLIPS)—a darkening of the sun or moon as either the moon or the Earth casts a shadow on the other

lens (LENZ)—a round piece of glass for gathering light in a telescope

lunar (LOON • er)—having to do with the moon

meteorite (MEE • tee • er • ite)—a piece of iron or rock that falls from space

observatory (ob • ZER • vuh • tore • ee)—a building with a large telescope for viewing objects in the sky

planet (PLAN • it)—a heavenly body that orbits a star and reflects the star's light

planetarium (plan • uh • TAIR • ee • um)—a building where an image of the night sky is projected overhead to show stars and planets and their movements

radio telescope (RAY • dee • oh TELL • uh • skope)—a telescope that picks up radio waves from the stars and planets

reflecting telescope (ree • FLECK • ting TELL • uh • skope)—a telescope that uses a mirror to gather light and focus it toward the viewer

refracting telescope (ree • FRACK • ting TELL • uh • skope)—a telescope that uses a glass lens to gather light and bend it toward the viewer

solar (SOH • ler)—having to do with the sun

solar system (SOH • ler SISS • tim)—the sun with the planets that revolve around it

spectroscope (SPECK • truh • skope)—an instrument that separates light into colors. It can be used to tell the age, distance, and makeup of stars.

star (STAHR)—a heavenly body that gives off its own light. Our sun is a star.

telescope (TELL • uh • skope)—a tube-shaped instrument that makes distant objects appear larger

universe (YOU • nih • verss)—everything there is, from the smallest particle to the largest star

visible (VIZ • ih • bil)—able to be seen

INDEX

PHOTO CREDITS

© Cameramann International, Ltd.—
Cover, 6 (bottom), 13 (top)

© Tony Freeman—4 (bottom)

Gartman Agency:
  © Photori—4 (top), 9 (top right),
17 (left), 29

Historical Pictures Services—9 (top left and bottom left)

Holiday Film Corp.—9 (bottom right),
20, 21 (2 photos), 25, 28 (right)

Journalism Services:
  © Dave Brown—18
  © Joseph Jacobson—8
  © J. Zietz—13 (bottom right)

Courtesy National Aeronautics and
Space Administration—10, 22

National Optical Astronomy
Observatories—26

Nawrocki Stock Photo:
  © Robert M. Lightfoot—19, 28 (left)
  © Paul P. Sipiera—6 (top)

Odyssey Productions:
  © Robert Frerck—15
  © Walter Frerck—17 (right), 27

Tom Stack & Associates:
  © Bill Tronca—23

Courtesy U.S. Naval Observatory—13
(bottom left)

ABOUT THE AUTHOR

Paul Sipiera is an Associate Professor of Physical Sciences at William Rainey Harper college in Palatine, Illinois, and a research associate in geology at the Field Museum of Natural History in Chicago. As a member of the National Science Foundation's Antarctic Research Program, he has studied geological features of the icy continent. Mr. Sipiera is technical advisor to Society Expedition's Project Space Voyage, the first venture into space for the general public. A teacher of astronomy and geology, his specialties are meteorites, moon rocks, and volcanoes. Mr. Sipiera gardens, grows vegetables, and plants maple trees at his home in Crystal Lake, Illinois.